D1141178

Licensed By:

First published in the UK by HarperCollins Children's Books in 2010

13579108642

978-0-00-736663-7

Transformers © 2010 Hasbro. All Rights Reserved. © 2010 DreamWorks, LLC and Paramount Pictures Corporation.
All Rights Reserved. General Motors trademarks licensed to Hasbro, Inc.

A CIP catalogue record for this title is available from the British Library.

No part of this publication may be reproduced, stored in a retrieval system or transmitted in any form or by any means,
electronic, mechanical, photocopying, recording or otherwise without the prior permission of HarperCollins Publishers
Ltd, 77-85 Fulham Palace Road, Hammersmith, London, W6 8JB.
All rights reserved.

Printed and bound in China

Written by Matt Crossick

TRANS FORMERS

ANNUAL 2011

CONTENTS

SAM IN DANGER – Part 1

Major Lennox jumped out of his chair and dashed over to one of the computer screens that filled the hi-tech NEST base. The screen was flashing red, and a large dot was blinking on a map of the world that filled the screen.

'Decepticons! In Japan!' he cried. 'Get me Optimus, now!'

The Major ran out of his office, and out onto a high platform in the huge aircraft hangar where NEST housed the Autobots. A deafening crashing,

clanking, scraping noise filled the room, before Optimus Prime's head peered over the top of the platform and looked straight at Major Lennox. 'Optimus!' cried the Major. 'We're getting reports of Decepticon activity over in Tokyo! We need you in action straight away!'

Optimus nodded, turned round, and issued a familiar command in his deep voice:

'Autobots – roll out!'

As he ran towards the hangar door, three more huge robots followed him: Ironhide, spinning his guns as he ran; Sideswipe, skating along on his wheeled feet; and Ratchet, still in disguise as a Hummer search and rescue truck.

The Autobots dashed out into the sunshine, switched to their vehicle disguises on the runway outside, and drove up a ramp into a huge Air Force aeroplane. Major Lennox jumped in after Ratchet, and team NEST were on the move!

As the Autobots, still in disguise, drove through the centre of Tokyo, they knew that the Decepticons weren't far away. Then Sideswipe screeched to a halt: there was something fishy about the police car they had just driven past. Sideswipe reversed slowly along the street, before jamming on his brakes: the police car was changing into a huge Decepticon at top speed!

Within seconds, the fearsome Barricade, Decepticon warrior, was charging towards Sideswipe, his guns blazing. People on the pavements ran screaming as Sideswipe quickly changed, and smashed into Barricade with an enormous crash. As the Autobot tried to use his sword arms to attack, Optimus Prime switched from his truck disguise and wrenched Barricade into the air with his incredible strength.

Optimus, however, suddenly crashed back to the ground, Barricade still in his hands: an attack helicopter was firing rockets at the Autobots from the sky above. Sideswipe dived for cover as explosions rained down and blew craters in the street.

'Sideswipe! Ratchet! Cover me!' boomed Optimus, jumping to his feet.

The two Autobots fired their guns at the helicopter as Optimus climbed the wall of an office block, storey by storey. As the helicopter fired back at Ratchet and Sideswipe, Optimus leaned out behind it, smashing it out of the sky with a fierce blow.

The helicopter, Grindor, tumbled out of the sky and smashed into Barricade, the two Transformers rolling down the street in a tangle of metal. Optimus jumped down and stood over them, his hands on his hips.

'Haven't you Decepticons learnt your lesson yet?' he boomed.

'Ha ha!' laughed Grindor, backing

away from Optimus. 'You didn't think we'd lose a fight like that for real, did you?' he cried. Changing back into a helicopter, he picked up Barricade and dashed up into the air.

'We just wanted to lure you over to the other side of the world!' Grindor cried. 'Our work here is done!'

Optimus and Sideswipe looked at each other as Major Lennox, in his army jeep, screeched to a halt at Optimus's feet.

'What's going on, Optimus?' he cried. 'Why did you let them go?'
Optimus frowned. 'It was a trap, Major!' he said. 'They wanted us out of America! Which means. . .'

The Major nodded. 'Sam! He must be in danger!'

Continued on p.20...

Spot the Difference

Bumblebee is armed, and ready to battle the Decepticons.
Can you spot the 5 differences between these two pictures of him?

Autobot Hunt

Optimus and the Autobots are trying to find
the Decepticons. Help them chase
Megatron through this shield maze!

Meet the Team: Autobots

The Autobots are our only hope in defending planet Earth!

Optimus Prime
Leader of the Autobots with one goal in mind: to protect the universe from the evil of Megatron. For this massive, metal warrior, nothing is more important than freedom; he will sacrifice all for its preservation.

Ratchet
Autobot medical officer, devoted to saving life, no matter what form it takes, and no matter whose it is.

Bumblebee
Autobot warrior sent to Earth to do what he does best: gather information, find the keeper of the secrets of the AllSpark and remain hidden. Bumblebee acts as an unseen guardian over his assigned target.

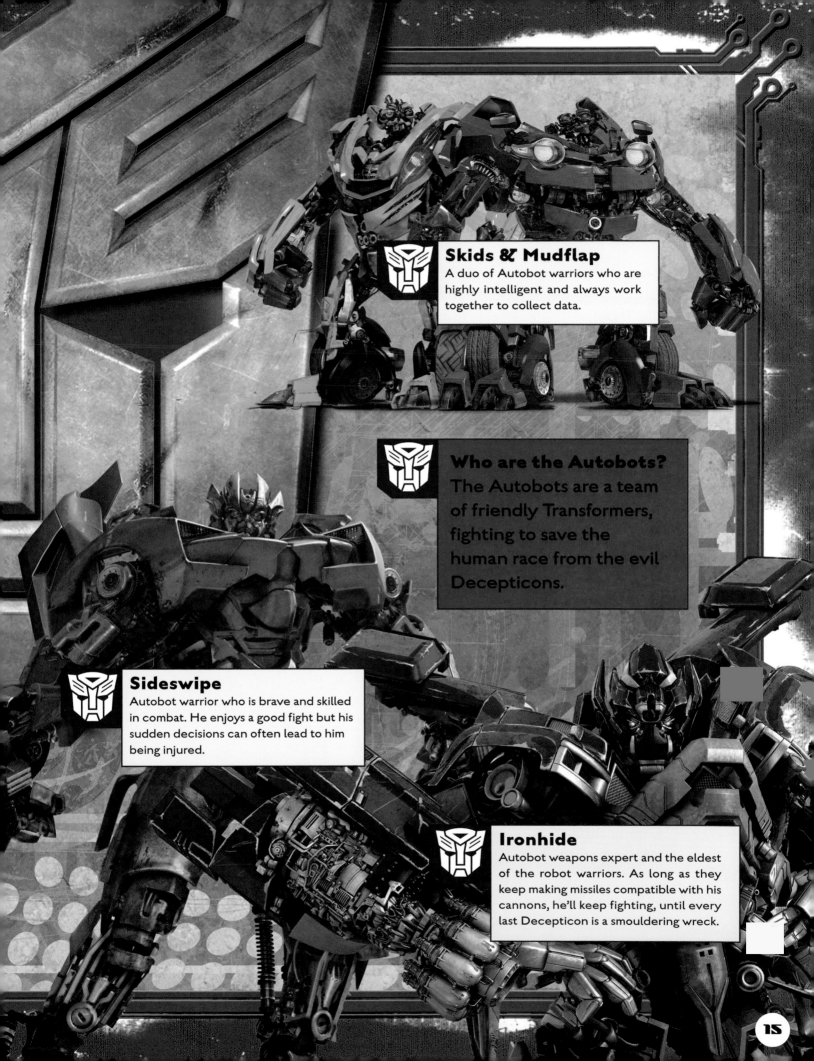

Skids & Mudflap
A duo of Autobot warriors who are highly intelligent and always work together to collect data.

Who are the Autobots?
The Autobots are a team of friendly Transformers, fighting to save the human race from the evil Decepticons.

Sideswipe
Autobot warrior who is brave and skilled in combat. He enjoys a good fight but his sudden decisions can often lead to him being injured.

Ironhide
Autobot weapons expert and the eldest of the robot warriors. As long as they keep making missiles compatible with his cannons, he'll keep fighting, until every last Decepticon is a smouldering wreck.

Bumblebee Puzzler

Take a look at the vehicles below.
Which one is Bumblebee in disguise?

1

2

3

4

5

6

Ironhide Attack

Ironhide has spotted some Decepticons and is about to open fire.
Finish the battle scene yourself with some coloured pens!

 Who is Ironhide fighting?
You can even make up a Decepticon
for him to battle if you like!

Hidden Autobots

The Autobots have gone under cover and are hiding in this wordsearch.
Can you find their names in the grid below?

V	U	E	V	S	V	C	W	M	O	I	O	T	U	P
J	Q	P	R	B	L	F	U	S	L	P	L	X	S	K
U	O	W	X	I	U	D	J	J	T	E	U	F	Y	H
L	J	O	Z	N	F	Q	B	I	I	U	D	Y	A	L
T	E	Z	Z	L	S	T	M	L	J	J	F	Y	A	L
Y	E	F	A	A	B	U	E	K	C	X	M	J	S	C
R	B	P	J	A	S	E	P	J	U	O	U	D	U	A
A	E	S	I	P	H	G	F	E	B	Q	X	F	B	O
T	L	K	R	W	Q	S	O	G	J	I	T	T	O	T
C	B	I	O	O	S	K	W	N	K	N	Q	W	T	S
H	M	D	N	Y	V	E	O	S	V	O	F	H	S	F
E	U	S	H	N	U	C	D	P	C	G	N	J	X	O
T	B	T	I	O	B	C	G	I	A	A	K	X	L	U
H	Y	L	D	O	Z	E	Z	M	S	T	J	A	V	Q
B	H	I	E	L	J	R	O	Y	J	I	A	P	K	L

Optimus Prime   **Mudflap**

Ironhide   **Jazz**

Bumblebee   **Jetfire**

Ratchet   **Wheelie**

Skids   **Sideswipe**

TRANSFORMER STATS NO.1

BUMBLEBEE

(Nickname:Bee)

Info:
Bumblebee is a brave, tough Autobot who continues to battle the Decepticons despite having his voicebox damaged in battle – he can only talk through his car radio now! He is fiercely loyal to Optimus and the other Autobots, as well as to Sam, who buys Bumblebee when he is disguised as a rusty old second-hand car.

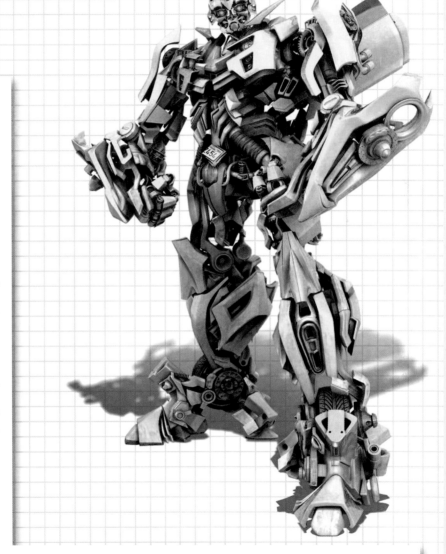

Height: 16.2 feet

Weight: 1.6 metric tons

Strength: Power Level 6

Weapons: Twin plasma canons

Job:
Personal bodyguard to Sam

Disguise:
Chevrolet Camaro sports car

SAM IN DANGER – Part 2

Sam sighed and put his pen down. Looking out of the window in front of his desk, he could see his father carefully planting flowers around the fountain in the middle of their perfect lawn. He was bored of doing his homework...he wondered if he could get away with taking Bumblebee for a ride before dinner.

As he reached into his desk for his car keys, a shadow fell across the window. The sound of his dad in the garden fell quiet, and a scraping, metallic noise replaced it. Sam looked up slowly. A huge, jagged, silver face filled the window.

'Aaaargh!' Sam cried, stumbling backwards and falling over his chair. 'Help!'

The face disappeared for a second, before a metal fist smashed through the wall and made a swipe for Sam.

'Bumblebee! Help!' Sam cried again, sprinting downstairs and running out towards the garage where he kept his personal Cybertronian bodyguard. Over his shoulder, he saw the Decepticon, Starscream gaining on him, his huge metal feet smashing his dad's garden to pieces as he stormed across the lawn.

But Sam didn't need to reach the garage: Bumblebee was already changing into battle mode and sprinting towards Starscream. The two Transformers met in the middle of the lawn with an almighty smash. Sam ducked behind a wall and peered out at the fight.

Bumblebee was pinning Starscream to the floor and preparing his guns for a killer blow, but the Decepticon was too strong for him. Starscream flung Bumblebee over his shoulder and opened fire with a rocket. Bumblebee attacked again, ripping at Starscream with his powerful hands, but again the Decepticon flung him across the garden and opened fire. A rocket whizzed past Sam's head, and Starscream dashed towards him.

With a roar, the Decepticon smashed the wall Sam was hiding behind to pieces, and grabbed Sam by the waist.

'Bumblebee! Do something!' yelled Sam, struggling against Starscream's grip.

Bumblebee bravely charged towards Starscream, but the huge Decepticon dodged him, and launched a rocket that sent him crashing into the garage. He set off down the street with Sam still gripped under his arm.

Sam looked back in despair as Starscream let out a horrible, screeching laugh – but it didn't last long. At the end of Sam's street, he saw a familiar pair of giant legs blocking Starscream's path.

'Optimus! Am I pleased to see you!' cried Sam, and Starscream froze. As Optimus leapt onto Starscream's back, wrestling him to the ground, Sam wriggled free and sprinted to safety.

Bumblebee charged into the fight too, and within seconds, Starscream was on the run. He struggled free of Optimus, changed into a jet, and flew into the sky with a furious roar.

'Thanks Optimus! Thanks Bumblebee!' said Sam, dusting himself down.

'You know we'll always be here for you, Sam!' growled Optimus.

Sam looked around him at the aftermath of the Transformers' battle. The front was ripped off his garage, and there was a fist-shaped hole punched in the wall of the house. The front garden was a mud-bath, with smashed pots, huge scars in the grass, and flakes of metal crushing the flowers his dad had just planted.

'I hope so, Optimus!' Sam replied, scratching his head. 'I think there's something scarier than Starscream after me right now!'

Optimus flexed his arms and loaded his guns. Bumblebee jumped up behind him.

'Really? Who?' the Autobot cried.

Sam laughed. 'My dad, when he sees this mess!'

Ravage Attack

Three Autobots are chasing Ravage. Which one gets to him first?

Ratchet

Sideswipe

Ironhide

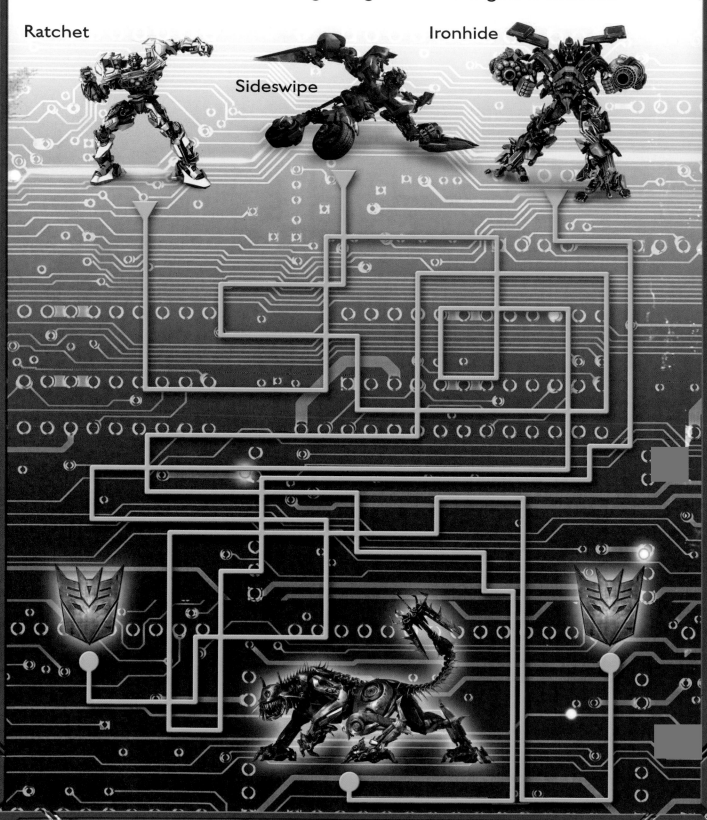

Word Pyramid

Read the clues and fill in the pyramid to stop The Fallen reaching the Star Harvester!

Clues:
1. The first letter of Bumblebee's nickname
2. The Autobot Leader's initials
3. The boy who helps the Autobots
4. Jet_____ gives his parts to Optimus
5. Mudflap's twin brother
6. The _____ is the evilest Decepticon
7. The opposite of a Decepticon

Re-arrange the letters in shaded boxes to reveal the final word in this sentence below.

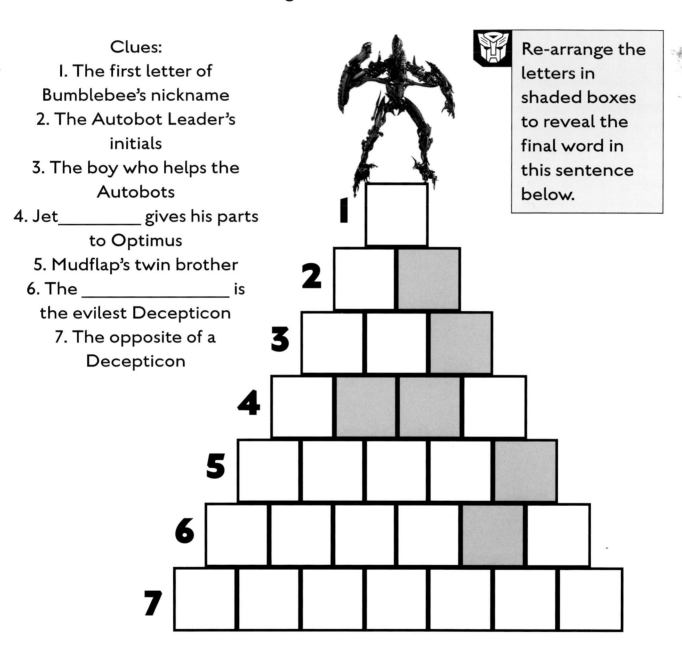

The Fallen can only be killed by a descendent of the _____

TRANSFORMER STATS NO.2
IRONHIDE

Info:
Ironhide is one of Optimus Prime's oldest friends and allies, and, after Optimus, is the toughest member of the Autobots team. He is a battle expert with fearsome weapons built into his arms, and has years of experience fighting the Decepticons. One thing is for sure, when the guns start blazing, you want Ironhide on your side!

Height: 22 feet

Weight: 2.4 metric tons

Strength: Power Level 8

Weapons: Ion-charged gatling

Job:
Autobots weapons expert

Disguise:
GMC SUV truck

Colour Ironhide

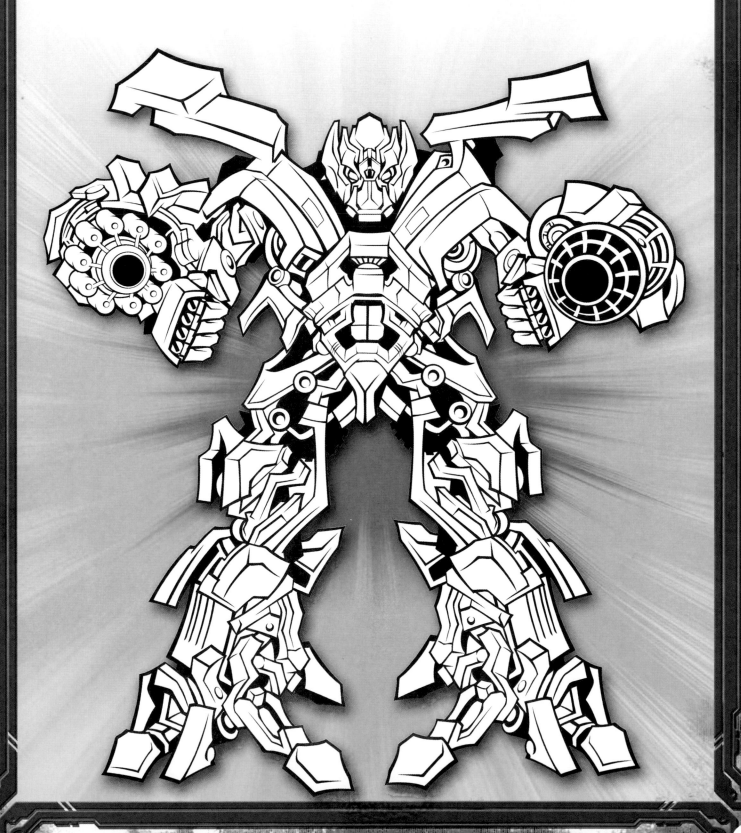

Optimus in Disguise

Optimus has shed his disguise and is ready for battle.
But can you spot the truck parts still dotted around his body?

Exhausts

Wheels

Doors

Windscreen

Roof panels

Wing mirror

Draw a line from each truck part to the place it appears on Optimus!

Ancient Code

Sam's head is full of ancient symbols again.
See if you can crack the language of the Primes and reveal the message!

A D E F H I L M O P R S T U V X

___ ___

_____ __

_____

__ _____

_____ _____

_____ _____

Meet the Enemy: Decepticons

These are the fearsome Decepticons threatening planet Earth!

Who are the Decepticons?

They are a group of evil Transformers, intent on destroying our sun – and the Earth with it – to create the energon they live on.

The Fallen

Megatron's master and the original Decepticon, who suffered a terrible fate and was sucked through a black hole into another dimension.

Starscream

Decepticon warrior and Megatron's right-hand man. His new authority means he punishes disobedience without mercy and rewards success only with a narrowed eye and threatening gesture.

Devastator
Giant destruction Decepticon – his sole purpose is to demolish anything and everything that gets in his way.

Ravage
Decepticon warrior who operates best alone. A creature of the night, Ravage performs most of his actions in the darkness.

Megatron
Leader of the Decepticons and the most dangerous Transformer ever to stalk the galaxy. He has no known weaknesses and only one purpose: to capture the AllSpark and rule the universe.

TRANSFORMER STATS NO.3
RATCHET

Info:

Ratchet is a search-and-rescue Transformer whose job it is to fix any Autobots injured in battle. He has laser vision, repair tools built into his arms, and travels with the team to help keep them safe – though even Ratchet can't revive Optimus Prime when he is killed by Megatron. Of course, Ratchet has some big guns built into his arms too, and he is happy to go into battle alongside the other Autobots.

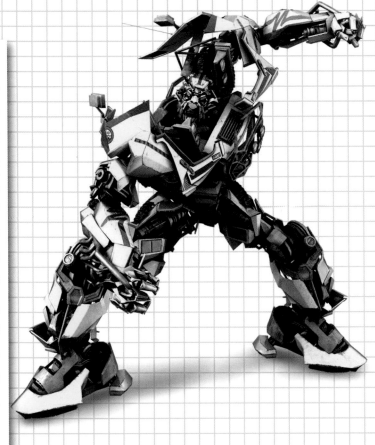

Stats:

Height: 20.1 feet

Weight: 2.3 metric tons

Strength: Power Level 4

Weapons: Detachable bi-directionable cutters

Job:
Autobots Medical Officer

Disguise:
Hummer Search and Rescue truck

Megatron Returns

Megatron has been revived with a splinter of the AllSpark!
Finish this picture of the Decepticon leader and colour it in.

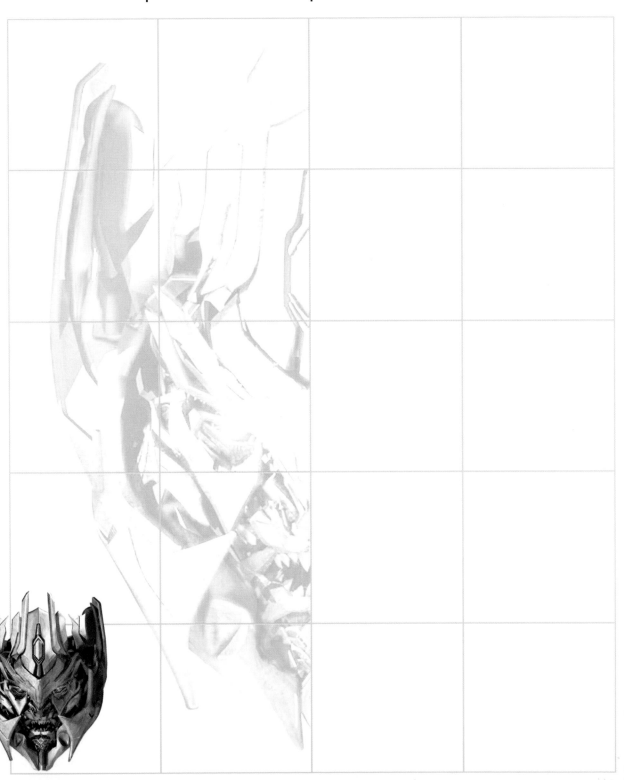

Transformer Shadows

Can you match each Transformer to its shadow?

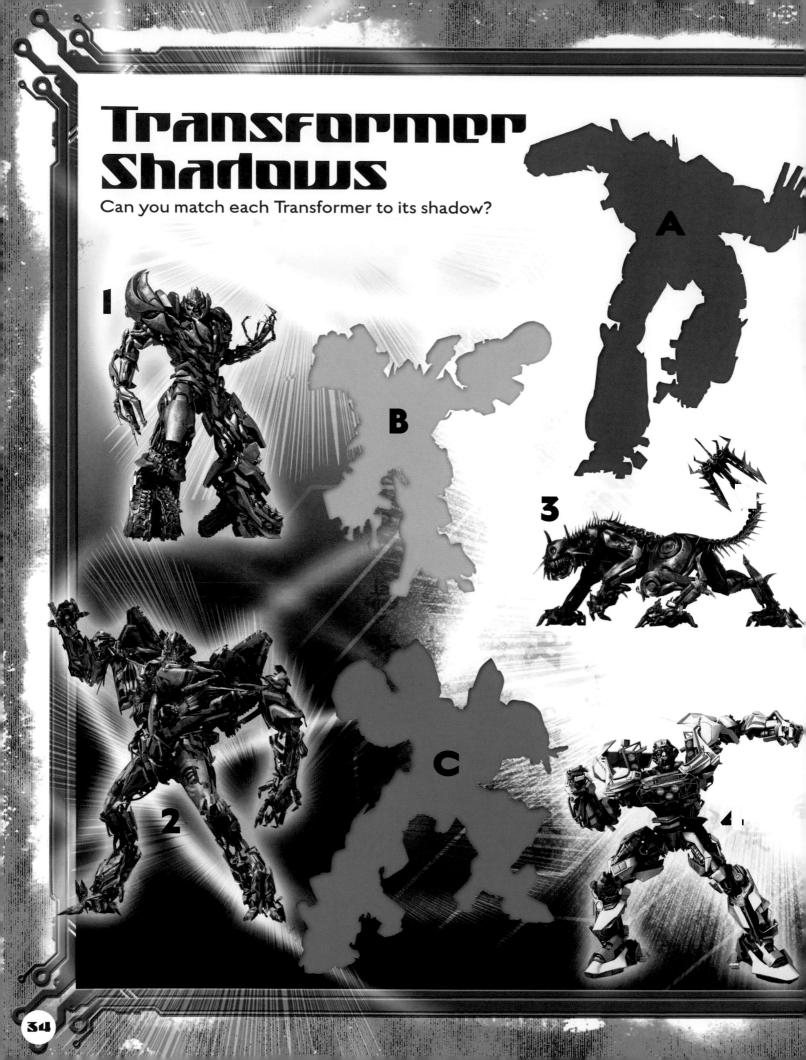

D

E

F

G

5

6

7

TRANSFORMER STATS NO.4
MEGATRON

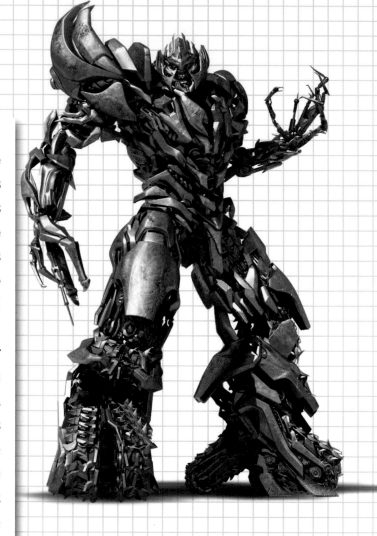

Info:

The leader of the Decepticons, Megatron is the most dangerous Transformer in the universe. He has a ruthless killer streak and a desire to see the human race wiped out – and he hates the Earth even more after being frozen in the arctic for thousands of years. Only Optimus Prime is tough enough to battle Megatron, and the Decepticon chief is still at large, waiting for his chance to attack again...

Stats:
Height: 35 feet
Weight: 5.7 metric tons
Strength: Power Level 10
Weapons: Ion-fused chain whip

Job:
Leader of the Decepticons

Disguise:
Cybertronian tank or jet

Devastator Maze

Devastator is getting even bigger by adding new machines to his body. Help him through the maze below, picking up each new body part on the way.

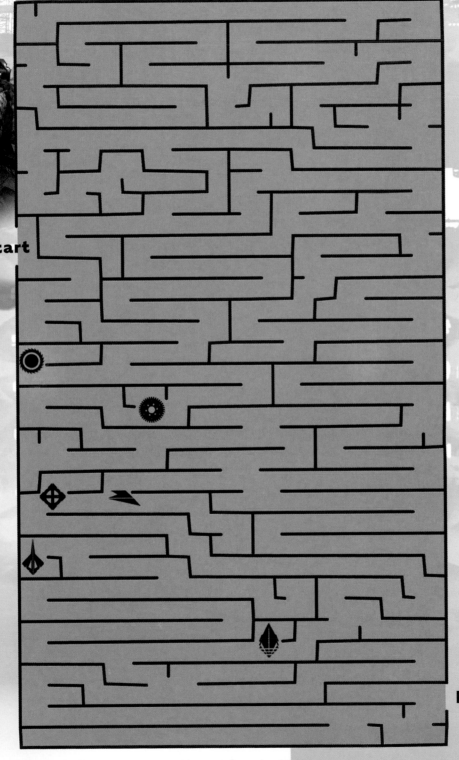

Start

Finish

The Tomb of the Primes Revealed

The mystery explained.

The Tomb of the Primes is a mystery at the heart of the battle between the Autobots and Decepticons.

Tens of thousands of years ago, when The Fallen first tried to harvest our sun and destroy the Earth, there was a battle between him and the powerful race of Primes (Optimus Prime's ancestors) in the desert. As the battle raged, the Primes realized that The Fallen was too strong for them, and couldn't be defeated.

They were determined to stop him, however, and made the ultimate sacrifice to save the Earth. The Fallen had built a Star Harvester, but needed a special key called the Matrix of Leadership to activate it. The Primes took the Matrix, and using their own bodies as a shield, sealed themselves together in a metal tomb with the Matrix inside – using their metal bodies to guard it forever, all of them dying in the process.

For thousands of years since, The Fallen has struggled to find the tomb, so that he could get the Matrix and harvest our sun. But the location was a mystery to everyone... until Sam started seeing strange symbols after he touched the fragment of the AllSpark.

The mysterious and ancient symbols were a clue to the location of the tomb; which is why The Fallen and Megatron needed Sam to find it. In the end, it is Skids and Mudflap's fighting that accidentally breaks through the wall of the tomb... and reveals the secret of the Primes after all these thousands of years.

The Matrix of Leadership
The Matrix is a key that activates the Star Harvester, which is why The Fallen is so desperate to find it. It has turned to dust since the Primes hid it in their tomb – but it still has the power to bring Optimus back to life; and it solidifies again after Sam revives him.

Transformers Masks

Recreate a Transformers battle with these Autobot and Decepticon masks!

What to Do
Trace each mask onto a clean sheet of paper. Cut the masks out, including eye holes. Colour your masks in the right colours. Attach some thin elastic to each mask to wear it!

See Optimus Prime and Megatron's Transformer Stats in this book to check which colours you should use!

TRANSFORMER STATS NO.5

DEVASTATOR

Info: Devastator is the biggest Decepticon the Autobots have had to battle so far. His huge bulk is made of lots of tough construction vehicles joined together, meaning that he is both super-strong and far bigger than other Transformers. He sucks up his enemies into his killer jaws to destroy them, and is the only Decepticon big enough to rip the top off the pyramid to reveal the Star Harvester.

Stats:
Intelligence: 2
Speed: 2
Strength: 10
Endurance: 10

Job:
Protect Megatron and reveal the Star Harvester

Disguise:
Splits into lots of smaller construction vehicles.

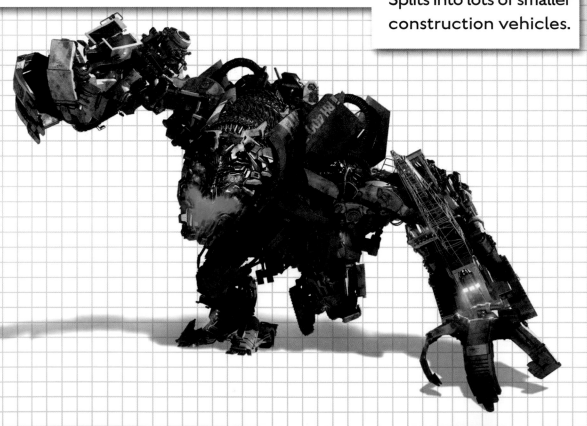

Skids & Mudflap's Joke Book

Why did the robot act crazy?
Because it had a screw loose.

What do robots eat for their dinner?
Micro chips.

How does a Transformer shave?
With a laser blade!

Do robots have sisters?
No, only transistors...

How do you get a spaceman's baby to sleep?
Rocket!

What do you call someone who draws funny pictures of vehicles?
A Car-toonist.

What's the laziest part of a truck?
The wheels. They're always 'tyred'.

When do cars always get flat tyres?
Wherever there's a fork in the road.

Where do aliens leave their spaceships?
At parking-meteors.

TRANSFORMER STATS NO.6
SIDESWIPE

Info:
Sideswipe is fast, agile and the warrior of the Autobot team. His wheeled feet mean that he can blast along at speed during battle, and his sword arms make him incredibly dangerous. He also has guns in his wrists and back. His biggest moment is chopping the Decepticon Sideways in half during a frantic chase in Shanghai.

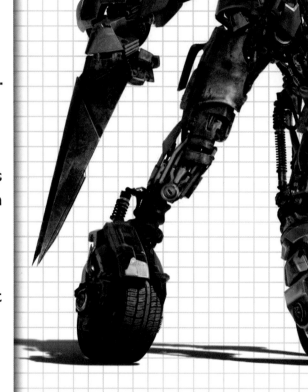

Stats:
Intelligence: 7
Speed: 8
Strength: 8
Endurance: 6

Job:
Autobot Warrior

Disguise:
Chevrolet Stingray concept car

Bumblebee in Disguise

There are clues to Bumblebee's disguise all over his body.
Can you spot the car parts below in this picture of him?

Rear wheels

Headlights

Exhaust

Car doors

Bumper

Front wheels

Number plate

Draw a line from each word to the right car part on Bumblebee's body!

Colour Megatron

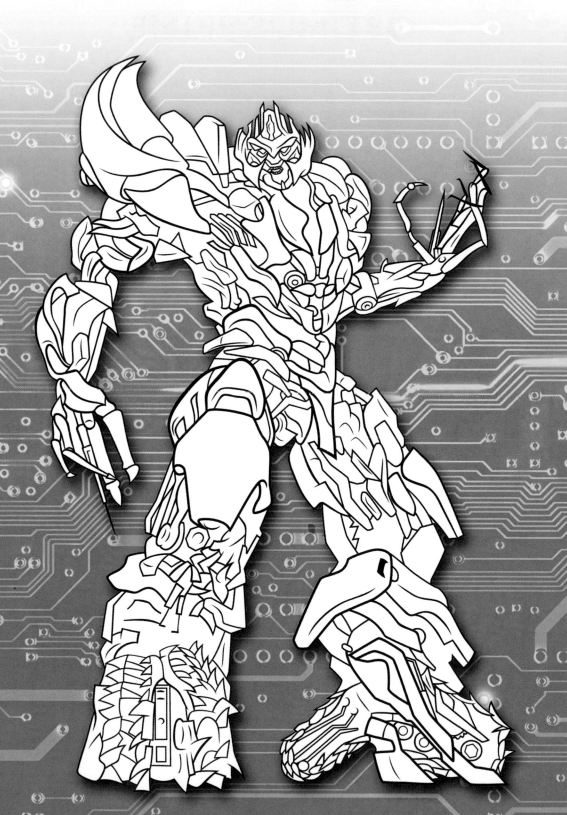

TRANSFORMER STATS NO.7
OPTIMUS PRIME

Info:
Optimus is the leader of the Autobots, and the final member of the ancient Prime family. He is a heroic, brave Transformer who came to Earth with his Autobot team to protect it from the Decepticons. Optimus is fearsome in battle, and the only Autobot strong enough to take on Megatron. Optimus becomes even more powerful when he uses Jetfire's wings and jets to finally bring down the Fallen.

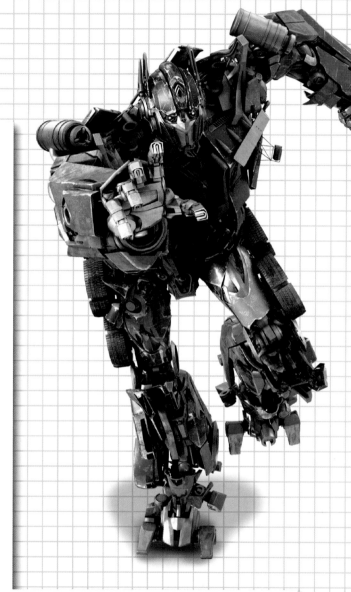

Stats:
Height: 28 Feet
Weight: 4.3 metric tons
Strength: Power Level 10
Weapons: Ion Blaster

Job:
Leader of the Autobots

Disguise:
Huge truck

The Story of The Fallen

Everyone on Earth thought that Megatron was the biggest, baddest Decepticon, and that they were safe with him buried at sea. But then they didn't know about THE FALLEN...

The Fallen is an ancient Transformer, and one of the original Primes. He set out with his comrades across the universe to find suns to harvest, tens of thousands of years ago, with only one rule to follow: they would never destroy a sun if it had planets with life on around it.

The Fallen, however, had other ideas. He didn't care about other life at all, and when he found Earth, he broke the golden rule and decided to try to harvest its sun, destroying the human race. 17,000 years ago he built a Star Harvester in the Egyptian desert, with the help of some other evil Transformers.

The other Primes came to Earth to stop them, and a great battle ensued. But The Fallen was a fearsome enemy. The Primes couldn't kill him – but they did seal away the 'key' to the Star Harvester (see 'The Tomb of the Primes Revealed', p.38), and they managed to imprison The Fallen. Although he was imprisoned, he could only be killed by a Prime.

When Megatron kills Optimus (the last Prime), however, The Fallen is freed from captivity. He escapes Cybertron, flies to Earth, and prepares to launch the Star Harvester once again, with the help of his new team of Decepticons. Of course, he isn't reckoning on Optimus Prime being brought back to life...

How dangerous is The Fallen?

Unlike newer Transformers, The Fallen doesn't have guns or rockets: he carries a long spear to fight with. He is, however, one of the most dangerous Transformers ever. He can teleport to wherever he wants, and release deadly shockwaves that kill anything in their path. He can also move objects with his mind, making him almost impossible to defeat in battle.

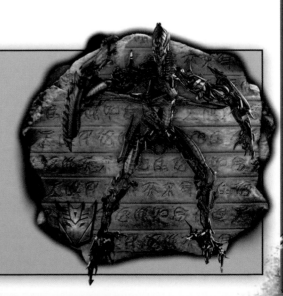

TRANSFORMER STATS NO.8
STARSCREAM

Info:

Starscream is one of the strongest Decepticons, and thanks to his ability to fly disguised as a jet, he is incredibly dangerous. He is Megatron's right-hand man, although his treacherous nature means that Megatron has to keep a close eye on him. He can travel faster than the speed of sound, uses his rockets as a jet pack when he is in battle mode, and, along with Megatron, he is one of the only Decepticons to survive the battle of the Star Harvester. Which means he could return at any time...

Stats:
Height: 31 feet
Weight: 2.6 metric tons
Strength: Power Level 7
Weapons: Plasma-charged rotor

Job:
Decepticon Air Commander

Disguise:
F-22 Raptor Airoplane

Decepticon Wordsearch

The Decepticons are laying low. Help the Autobots reach them by finding their names in this wordsearch!

X	W	O	X	M	F	X	W	Z	R	M	N
Y	Z	F	M	A	G	B	D	O	U	E	E
P	N	P	W	E	Z	T	T	X	S	G	L
D	Y	U	S	R	G	A	G	I	W	A	L
L	G	E	U	C	T	A	D	G	N	T	A
P	V	G	I	S	O	E	V	W	G	R	F
M	H	I	A	R	W	R	A	A	X	O	E
P	I	V	V	A	C	Z	P	J	R	N	H
V	E	B	Y	T	O	D	U	O	M	R	T
D	Q	S	K	S	S	N	Q	N	N	E	J
S	O	U	N	D	W	A	V	E	H	O	S
R	O	D	N	I	R	G	U	T	Z	J	K

Megatron	Ravage	Soundwave
Starscream	The Fallen	Scorponok
Devastator	Grindor	Sideways

Hidden Parts

The Autobots need to find some spare parts to get ready for a big battle.
Can you find the following pieces hidden in the picture below?

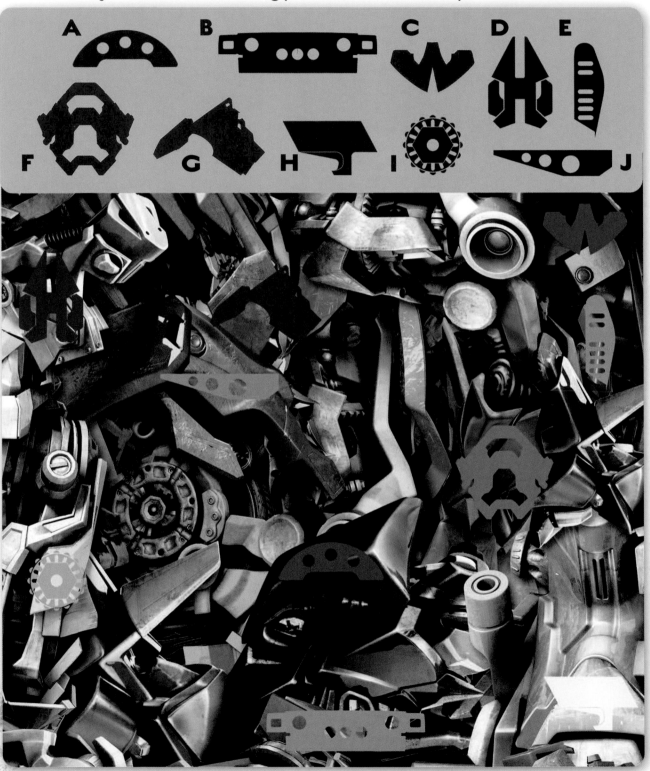

TRANSFORMER STATS NO.9

SKIDS & MUDFLAP

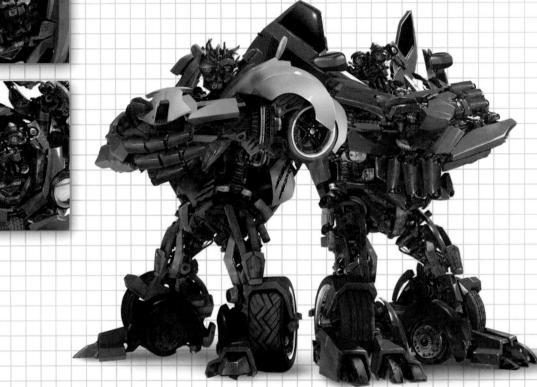

Info:

Skids and Mudflap are two twins who can't stop arguing with each other – but whose near-psychic link with each other means that they are great in battle. Their original disguise was a battered ice-cream truck, but they swapped it for two cool concept cars, which suit their street style.

Skids stats:	**Mudflap stats:**	**Job:**
Intelligence: 6	**Intelligence:** 5	Autobot warriors
Speed: 7	**Speed:** 7	
Strength: 4	**Strength:** 4	**Disguise:**
Endurance: 4	**Endurance:** 5	Concept cars

Optimus Vs. Megatron

Who will win the ultimate Transformer battle?

Size:		
Strength:		
Power:		
Speed:		
Weapon Strength:		
Disguise:		
Bravery:		
Intelligence:		
Fighting Skill:		Total:
Toughness:		

What to do

Fill in each stat out of ten in the boxes provided, depending on how good you think each Transformer is at that skill.

Add up each Transformer's total points in the box at the bottom. The Transformer with the highest total is the winner!

Size:	
Strength:	
Power:	
Speed:	
Weapon Strength:	
Disguise:	
Bravery:	
Intelligence:	
Fighting Skill:	Total:
Toughness:	

The winner is:

Crack the Pattern

Optimus is trying to crack a Decepticon pattern.
Help him out by colouring the final symbol in each row the right colour!

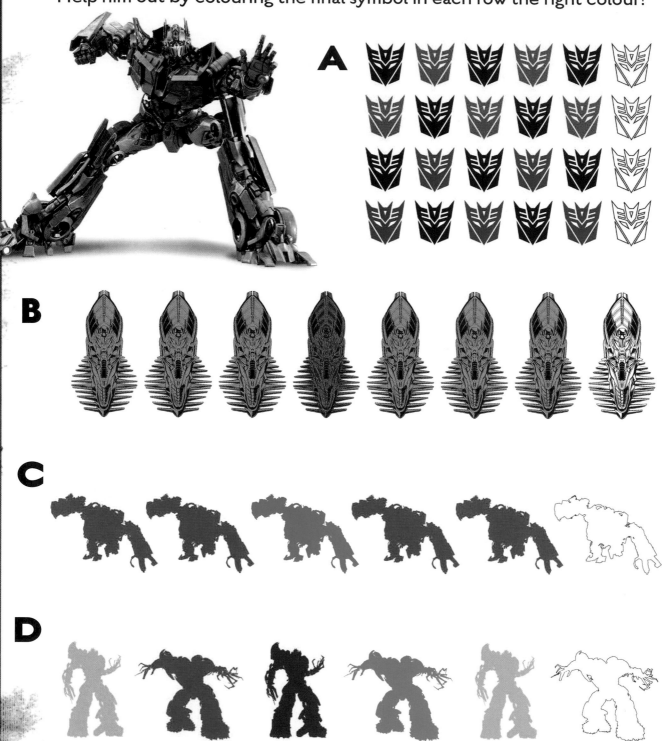

A

B

C

D

TRANSFORMER STATS NO.10
THE FALLEN

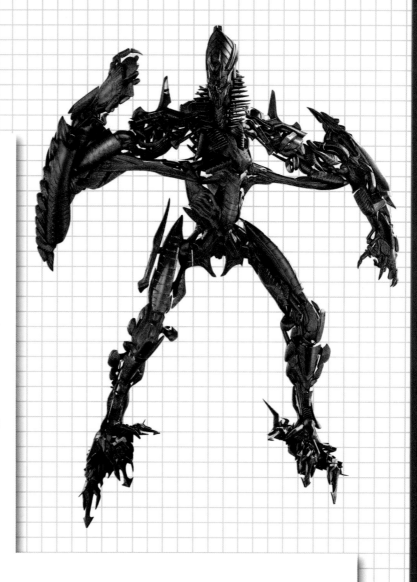

Info:

Thousands of years old, The Fallen was imprisoned after he tried to destroy humanity in ancient times. He is determined to destroy humanity by turning the Star Harvester on our sun, and only Optimus Prime can stop him. The Fallen is the true leader of the Decepticons and the only Transformer that Megatron will obey; and his incredible internal power can be used as a shockwave to kill his enemies.

Job:

One of the original Primes and the original Decepticon chief

Disguise:

None

Transformers Quiz

How much have you learned about Transformers by reading this annual?
Take this tricky quiz to find out!

**1. What is the name of
the Transformers' home planet?**
Cybertron
Mars
Transformatron

**2. Which device was Megatron
looking for when he crashed into
the ice?**
A new spaceship
Optimus Prime
The AllSpark

**3. What is
Bumblebee's nickname?**
Bumble
Bee
Stripes

4. True or false:
The Fallen is the
true leader of the Decepticons

5. Which Transformer is disguised as a Search and Rescue Hummer?
Ratchet
Ironhide
Sparks

6. What does the Matrix of Leadership do?
Kills Decepticons
Teleports Transformers
Activates the Star Harvester

7. What is the only thing that can kill The Fallen?
A descendent of the Primes
The US Army
Sam

8. Which Decepticon is this?

9. Who is the Autobot weapons expert?
Ratchet
Sideswipe
Ironhide

10. What is the leader of the Autobots called?
Megatron
Optimus Prime
Ratchet

Check your answers on page 61, then fill in your score here!

/10

Answers

p.12

p.13

p.16

Bumblebee is car *5*

p.18

V	U	E	V	S	V	C	W	M	O	I	O	T	U	P
J	Q	P	R	B	L	F	U	S	L	P	L	X	S	K
U	O	W	X	I	U	D	J	J	T	E	U	F	Y	H
L	J	O	Z	N	F	Q	B	I	I	U	D	Y	A	L
T	E	Z	Z	L	S	T	M	L	J	J	F	Y	A	L
Y	E	F	A	A	B	U	E	K	C	X	M	J	S	C
R	B	P	J	A	S	E	P	J	U	O	U	D	U	A
A	E	S	I	P	H	G	F	E	B	Q	X	F	B	O
T	L	K	R	W	Q	S	O	G	J	I	T	T	O	T
C	B	I	O	O	S	K	W	N	K	N	Q	W	T	S
H	M	D	N	Y	V	E	O	S	V	O	F	H	S	F
E	U	S	H	N	U	C	D	P	C	G	N	J	X	O
T	B	T	I	O	B	C	G	I	A	A	K	X	L	U
H	Y	L	D	O	Z	E	Z	M	S	T	J	A	V	Q
B	H	I	E	L	J	R	O	Y	J	I	A	P	K	L

p.24

Sideswipe gets to Ravage first!

p.25

1. B
2. O.P
3. Sam
4. Fire
5. Skids
6. Fallen
7. Autobot

Hidden
word:
Primes

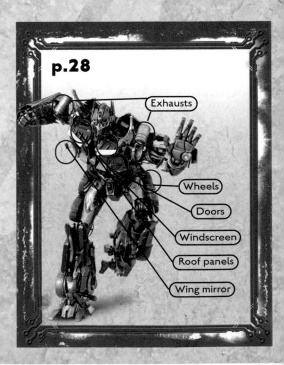

p.28

Exhausts

Wheels

Doors

Windscreen

Roof panels

Wing mirror

p.29

The code reads: "Use the Matrix of Leadership to revive Optimus Prime"

p.34

1=G, 2=E, 3=F, 4=D, 5=A, 6=D, 7=B

p.37

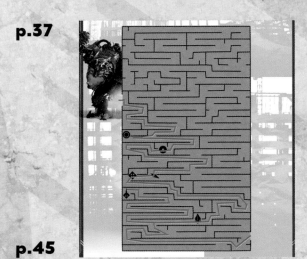

p.45

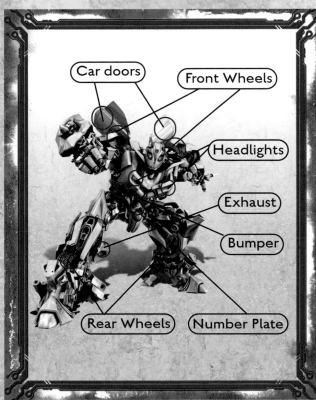

Car doors

Front Wheels

Headlights

Exhaust

Bumper

Rear Wheels

Number Plate

p.51

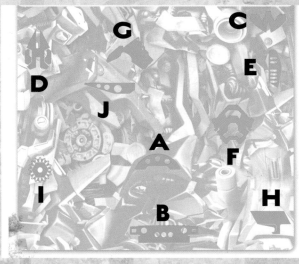

p.52

p.56

A. Red, B. Black, C. Blue, D. Black

p.60

1.Cybertron, 2.The Allspark, 3. Bee 4.True, 5. Ratchet, 6. Activates the Star Harvester, 7. A Descendent of the Primes, 8. Starscream, 9. Ironhide 10. Optimus Prime